Getting Better Grades:

*A Strategic Approach for
Inside and Outside the Classroom*

JIMMIE F GLORIOSO JR

ISBN: 1490479252

ISBN 13: 9781490479255

Library of Congress Control Number: 2013911794

CreateSpace Independent Publishing Platform

North Charleston, South Carolina

Table of Contents

Part I:

Setting the Stage

CHAPTER 1

Introduction

I decided to write this book in order to help the millions of students (and/or parents of students) who are not satisfied with their grades. The strategies and techniques that I will share with you are applicable to middle and high school students as well as undergraduate and graduate students. In fact, they can be used for any classroom or training environment.

Although I was always self-motivated, I was not nearly as intelligent or gifted as a number of my peers in the classroom. However, I did always work as hard, or in some cases harder, than they did. This is demonstrated by the fact that although I was not a National Merit Finalist or even Semi-Finalist, I was Valedictorian of my high school class. I applied to six colleges and universities (Tulane University, Louisiana State University, University of Loyola (New Orleans), Millsaps College, Rhodes College, and the University of Notre Dame) and received scholarship offers from all six of them. I am also proud of the fact that I have never received a "C" or lower on any report card from elementary school through graduate school.

As I observed the classroom behaviors and study habits of my peers over the years, I began to realize what separated me from the rest of the pack. As I pondered it further, it made sense to me to compile a list of all those things that gave me an edge in the classroom and this book is the result of it. One theme that you will see stressed over and over again is "quality over quantity". I was not the student who studied more or longer than everyone else. My idea was to be as efficient as possible and make the most of all of the time I spent inside the classroom. I have used these techniques and strategies myself during middle school, high school, college (both undergraduate and graduate), and continue to do so even today when studying for certifications in the information technology field.

While I feel awkward talking about my achievements, I feel compelled to do so in order for you to understand how the strategies and techniques have paid off for me. I also would like to take a moment to say that academia was just one of many priorities for me. While I pushed myself to be the best I could be inside the classroom, I would like to mention that I did so while participating in many extra-curricular activities including football, baseball, and basketball as well as student council, prom committee, etc. Because middle, high school, and college extra-curricular activities are so time consuming, it was even more important for me to get the most of the time spent inside and outside the classroom.

I graduated with honors from Rhodes College with a Bachelor of Science degree in Biology with a 3.67 GPA. I did this while playing quarterback for the football team and throwing the javelin for the track and field team. Rhodes had a very challenging curriculum and without my study habits and classroom strategies, I would have never been able to be this successful academically, participate in all of these activities, and still have time for a social life. Several years later, I entered graduate school at the University of Texas at Dallas, where I attained my Master of Science degree with a perfect GPA of 4.0 in Information Technology and Management. I did this while holding a full-time job and raising twin preschoolers. Again, I really needed to study "smarter" and not longer as there were not enough hours in the day to study using the traditional methods.

While I hesitate to guarantee results, I am positive that if you use my techniques and strategies, you will see marked improvement in your grades. Your ability to retain information will be greater and you will most likely be able to study "less" since you will be grasping more from your time spent in school. In addition, you will find that you will be less stressed and have more time for the fun activities in your life.

Good luck and I look forward to hearing your success stories!

CHAPTER 2

Commitment

The first step to accomplishing anything in life is to wholeheartedly commit to it. Look at yourself in the mirror and tell yourself that you will commit to trying these techniques for the next year, semester, or at least 9 weeks. Commitment is a mindset. It requires you to fixate on the end goal and to stay the course. When you are truly committed to something, only extraordinary circumstances should prevent you from keeping that commitment.

Commitment also means never giving up. You WILL have setbacks from time to time. The key is to not get discouraged and to learn from each and every experience, both good and bad. Making good grades is no different than accomplishing any other task. You have to truly "care" about it and put in the time and effort it takes to get the job done well.

Being committed also means not worrying about what others think. There WILL be times when your friends think you are crazy. They will be the same friends that cannot believe that you outscored them on an exam when they studied twice as long as you did. The first thing you need to do is commit yourself to reading this book in its entirety (which should not be very difficult considering its length). Sure, there are a couple of items here or there that you can pull out and use to your advantage. However, it is the combination of all these techniques that will allow you to achieve maximum results, with the least amount of time investment.

There are some studies out there that suggest you should study 3 hours for every hour you spend in the classroom. In my mind, this is absurd. A typical high school day consists of a minimum of 5-6 hours of classroom time (excluding lunch, physical education, etc.). In order to follow what the studies suggest, a high school student would have to study for 15-18 hours that night, which we all know is practically impossible. Even if you only studied for 6 hours, there would be little or no time for extra-curricular activities, jobs, hobbies, fun, Facebook, Instagram, Twitter, etc. let alone sleep. The key is to truly make the most of every single minute spent in the classroom. Since you have to be there anyway, it would be foolish not to take this approach. This alone will save you hours and hours of study time at home.

I would like to end this chapter with a few thoughts that come to mind when thinking about commitment. One is "Commitment to Excellence". This is the mantra of the late Al Davis, former owner and general manager of the Oakland Raiders of the National Football League. Although the Raiders have not always played well on the field, everyone knew Al's commitment level. As an NFL owner, he was willing to do whatever it took to put a quality product on the football field. This "whatever it takes" attitude goes hand in hand with commitment. You must be committed to the classroom. You need to will your way to doing whatever needs to be done to get the results that you want. While you will never achieve perfection, your consistent pursuit of it will bring you more reward and satisfaction than you ever had before. Once you make this "commitment", you are ready to put the techniques and strategies explained throughout this book into action.

Part II:
Inside the Classroom

CHAPTER 3

Location, Location, Location!

We have all heard that location is everything when it comes to real estate. Imagine two identical houses and place one on beach front property and the other in a downtrodden part of town. Their values will be hundreds of thousands of dollars apart. How can this be? We are talking about the same house. It all has to do with your surroundings.

In my experience, a similar thing can be said of the classroom. The quality of the instruction that you receive is tied in many ways to your physical location in the classroom. Although every student is in position to hear the same things, learn the same subjects, and participate equally in discussions, it is greatly influenced by location. There are two major factors when discussing the importance of location in the classroom: distance from the teacher/professor and those who surround you.

Let's start with the first one. One of the most important things you can do in the classroom is to sit as close to the front as possible. This has many advantages. First, since you are physically closer, you will be able to hear the instructor more clearly and easily see any visual aids such as projected images on a screen or even a whiteboard. Second, and almost as important, sitting in front of the classroom gives an impression to the instructor that you are interested in what he/she is talking about. This can play a huge role in your grades, especially if class participation represents a portion of your grade. As a former teacher myself, I recognized that in those cases where students got to choose where they sit, the more interested students sat in the front while the others sat in the back. As always, there were a few exceptions, but overall, this was definitely the trend.

I understand in middle school and even in high school that students do not always have a choice when it comes to where they sit. If this is the case, you can always appeal to the instructor or even have a parent request that you be moved closer to the front of the class so that you can better hear/see what the instructor is saying/doing. In college, this is most often not an issue as almost all classes are "open" seating, meaning you can sit wherever you would like. While attending college, it always amazed me how, on the first day of class, 75% of the students would sit at least ten rows back from the professor and really struggle to read his notes on the board or hear what he had to say. It does not take a genius to know that if you cannot see or hear what is going on, your chances of doing well in that class are pretty minimal at best.

As I mentioned earlier, physical location in relation to the instructor is just one factor when it comes to location in the classroom. The other factor, which is equally important, is your physical location in relation to those around you. That is, who are the people sitting in front of, adjacent to, or behind you? Are they your friends? Are they trouble makers? Are they class clowns? These are all examples of the folks near whom you do NOT want to sit. The trouble makers and class clowns make sense, right? They are a constant source of distraction and will often cause you to lose your concentration. On the other hand, what about your friends?

While your friends are some of the most important people in your life, sitting next to them in class will NOT help you. While there are rare occasions where folks can be successful sitting next to their friends, I have been most successful when not sitting with them. This is not easy and sometimes it takes a fairly difficult conversation with your friends to explain why you do NOT want to sit with them. Remember what I said earlier. The key is to maximize your time spent in the classroom. If you sit with your friends, you will always be tempted to talk about various topics, goof off, discuss upcoming weekend plans, etc. If you surround yourself with folks whom you do not know or care for, you will be much more likely to pay attention and know what is going on in class. Reducing the possibility and frequency of distraction is paramount. I learned this the hard way with my first Biology class in college. I started off the class sitting in the back of the auditorium with a bunch of my friends from the football team and from the dorm. We were always cutting up and laughing in class. While it was fun, it was impacting my retention of the material and on my first exam I scored a 75, which did NOT make me happy. The next week, I moved down a couple of rows and my grade on the next exam improved quite a bit.

As you can imagine, the peer pressure you will get regarding where you sit in class can be immense and trying to make your friends understand why you do not want to sit with them can be challenging. One way to explain it is to let them know that by not sitting with them inside class; it will allow you to spend more time with them outside class. You have to go to school anyway, so the more you get out of being in class, the less time you have to spend at home reviewing the material. As a result, you will have more "free" time at home to do what you want, which includes hanging out with those same friends.

In summary, if you sit near the front of the class and surround yourself with people who are not distractions, you will have taken two huge steps in improving your concentration, retention, and ultimately, your success in the classroom.

CHAPTER 4

Questions Anyone?

Nobody enjoys being the student who asks the stupid question in class and then becomes the target for ridicule. However, asking good questions is critical to learning in the classroom. By not asking questions in class, you are giving up a great opportunity to clarify what you may or may not have learned regarding the particular topic at hand. In addition, because most subject matter builds off previous topics, you will find yourself falling behind and by not getting your questions answered; you may find yourself totally lost very quickly. The rule that I follow is to never leave class with questions about or a lack of clarity regarding a particular topic. I strongly encourage you to do the same.

As I have stated a couple of times earlier and will continue to do so throughout this book, you cannot be concerned with what others think. When in the classroom, you cannot be afraid to ask questions regardless of how shy you may be. If you are paying attention, odds are that your question will be a good one. In addition, by getting your question answered, you will feel much better about the subject matter and will leave class with confidence instead of leaving class wondering what the instructor was talking about. In addition, it is also highly likely that some of your classmates probably had the same question and by you asking it, you have helped them out as well.

In my mind, there is no such thing as a dumb question, that is, as long as it has something to do with the topic. As a former teacher myself, and as a husband of a teacher, I believe most teachers/professors would agree with me. In most cases, the teacher will answer your question and move right along. In some cases though, it may be a little more involved and he/she may ask you to stay after class or to come by before or after school, or even at lunch to get a little more instruction on the topic. Although this may be inconvenient, it is something that is absolutely necessary to make the grade. The 15 or 30 minutes of inconvenience could be the difference between a high "A" and a "C" or lower. As stated earlier, if you are committed, you will do what it takes to get the job done and this is just another one of those things. It may even mean telling your friends "no".

For example, let's say your friends want to eat lunch with you to talk about some upcoming weekend plans, but you just left Algebra class and really don't understand "slope" or how to apply the various formulas to find it. You asked a couple of questions in class, but the teacher replied by saying she really needed to get through the subject matter in class and that you could come by during lunch for a more thorough explanation. It WOULD be difficult to tell your friends that you will not be able to join them for lunch today. However, in the grand scheme of things, it really is not that big of a deal. You can always catch up with them later. The extra few minutes spent with the teacher will pay big dividends come test time.

When it comes to asking questions in class, I would be lying if I told you that I was always comfortable with it. However, over time, it became easier and easier the more times that I did it. Moreover, there were very few times, if any, that I would receive snickers or laughs from others in class. Actually, in most cases, I think they were thankful that I asked the questions that I did. It clarified things for them when they were too shy or uncomfortable with asking similar questions themselves.

This principle applies for almost anything we do in life. From middle and high school, to college, to jobs in the "real world", to appointments with your physician, auto mechanic, etc., asking questions is a fundamental way to learn and understand the world around you. When it comes to your job, you absolutely need to be able to ask your boss questions. If you don't, and later fail because you didn't understand something, it could cost you your job. When it comes to your health, it is essential that you ask your physician questions to better understand your body and what is or isn't functioning correctly and why. I do the same thing when it comes to service calls at my house. While I don't claim to be an expert in the fields of mechanics, carpentry, electronics, plumbing, etc., I know a great deal more now than I did as a kid because I ask tons of questions when repair men or installers come to my house to troubleshoot or install things.

As you can tell, I cannot stress enough the importance of asking questions. It will help you tremendously in the classroom and you will feel much more confident in your understanding of the subject matter. It is such a good feeling to walk out that door when the bell rings (I know I am dating myself here) knowing you have a good grasp of what was just covered. In addition, as you will see later, this will greatly reduce the amount of time required when studying for quizzes, tests, and exams. In this case, you will be reviewing the knowledge you thoroughly understood DURING class instead of still trying to figure things out AFTER it.

CHAPTER 5

Note Taking

Starting in the seventh or eighth grade, taking good notes is the most important thing you can do in the classroom. Note taking is more than just writing down information. It is an art form in and of itself. The goal of note taking is to write down the important items covered in class so that when reviewed, you will easily be able to remember the context in which the material was presented and be able to demonstrate this knowledge on quizzes, tests, and exams. Although there is a good deal of literature out there on note taking, I will share with you what has worked for me and why I believe it has proved to be so successful.

As I mentioned earlier, these various strategies build upon one another. In order to take good notes, you need to be close enough to hear the instructor and see what he/she is writing on the whiteboard or displaying via the projector. In addition, you need to be in a location where you can fully concentrate on the material being presented. Try to limit any and all distractions. Once these conditions are satisfied, you are ready to take good notes.

Note taking is NOT writing down everything the teacher/professor says. While that would be helpful, it is extremely difficult to do, would eventually hurt your hand and fingers, and could actually make study time longer as you would have to fish through all of the fluff in order to get to the substance. In order to take good, meaningful notes, you need to be able to decipher what should and shouldn't be written down. This will differ from one teacher to the next. There are those teachers whose lectures are made up of almost entirely testable information. In this case, almost all of the information is good and it is much more difficult to determine what NOT to write down. However, there are also those teachers who are storytellers and add a lot of filler information that isn't necessary to retain at a detailed level. In those classes, you need to be able to quickly determine when they go off on a tangent, and when they come back to the material at hand.

There are also a number of written and verbal cues that instructors will use that are "absolutes" when it comes to writing things down. When these things are done, you can almost guarantee that these items will show up on an exam in one form or another. It is quite obvious that when an instructor says "you need to know this", "this will be on the test", or "expect to see this again", you definitely need to write these things down in your notes. However, instructors sometimes use more subtle ways of demonstrating the importance of certain items during class and it is important to look/listen for these cues during each and every class.

If an instructor repeats himself two or more times when mentioning a particular topic in class, then it is highly likely that you will see it again. If he/she takes the time to write something on the board, you need to write it down as well. In some cases, the instructor will underline or circle something on the board. Again, this is an indicator that it will be covered on an exam. On the other hand, they can be extremely helpful and explicitly tell you that a particular topic will NOT be covered on an exam and that the following information is just for your "edification and/or amusement" as my English IV teacher once put it. These are welcome words to your ears, especially if it has been an intense note taking day. Put you pencil or pen down and simply enjoy the break.

Another key to good note taking is being organized. Always date your notes so that you can go back later and know when certain topics were covered. Write legibly so that when you go back to study your notes, you can actually read what you wrote. This has bitten me on a couple of occasions and I had to learn the hard way. I can recall on more than one occasion thinking to myself "what in the world did I write down". Try not to doodle within your notes. If the temptation gets the best of you, use the margins so that your fine artwork does not intermingle with the "substance". Another important tactic is to find ways to abbreviate or use symbols when taking notes. On many occasions, it will be very difficult to keep up with what the instructor is saying. As a result, you need to figure out ways to write less and still maintain the integrity of what you are writing (or in some cases typing).

One thing you can do is use symbols. For example, you can use the Greek delta "D" for the word "change". You can use three dots in the shape of a triangle for the word "therefore". There are countless other symbols you can use to shorten the amount of material you need to jot down. Using abbreviations or initials was another tactic that I found to be extremely helpful. When taking notes on names, countries, treaties, wars, etc., I would write down an abbreviation next to the phrase the first time I wrote it and then, every time I needed to reference that name or phrase, I would just use the abbreviation or initials. For example, in a History class, I may jot down the Treaty of Versailles. In my notes I would write "ToV" next to it and then I would use those three letters throughout my notes to reference back to the Treaty mentioned earlier. That would save me 14 characters every time I referenced that phrase. With names, it is even easier. Let's say we are studying Science and we are covering Louis Pasteur. Just jot down an LP next to his name and then refer to him as LP throughout the rest of your notes. Using this technique will save you lots of time and will also reduce your chances of missing something said, since you will be writing less and listening more.

When possible, it is really important that you try to write down as much of the relevant information as you can. Science suggests that you retain information better by writing information down when compared to just listening to it. In addition, you will have something to review when studying for the exam as opposed to just relying on memory. Although I strongly rec-ommend writing down as much as you can, it is equally import to identify those KEY points for which you really need to focus. I always did this by underlining the particular words, placing an asterisk by an item, or circling it. These are the items you will review over and over again whereas you may just read through the rest of your notes a couple of times in preparation for an exam.

In conclusion, quality note taking is something that will take time and practice. Over time, you should be able to write down more and more information by using less and less ink by using some of the techniques described above. In addition, if you mark your notes to identify the most important points, you will be sure to focus your attention on the most important top-ics when exam time approaches. As mentioned earlier, your ability to take good notes increases dramatically if you are in a good position to hear and see the instructor and if you are free from distractions. In addition, it is imperative that you ask questions if something doesn't make sense either during class or when you are reviewing your notes. Last, you must be com-mitted to paying attention and blocking out all other thoughts until class is over.

Part III:

Outside the Classroom

CHAPTER 6

Homework

Homework is one of those necessary evils that no student enjoys. As much as we would like to deny it, much of the reinforcement of the skills we learn in the classroom occurs via this route. Homework is important for a number of reasons. First, it gives us an opportunity to find out how well we know the material. Second, in most classes, it counts as a portion of our grade. Third, it prepares us for quizzes and exams. In many cases, credit is given for just doing the homework. As a result, it is purely asinine to not do it.

Let us examine the first point in more detail. In my opinion, homework is a win-win opportunity. If you complete your homework with no problems (no pun intended), then you can be confident that you know the material and only a little review will be needed for the test. However, more importantly, if you struggle with any part of the homework, you know exactly what you need to ask your instructor the next day in class. As discussed in a previous chapter, you absolutely need to do this. If you have questions or concerns but never discuss them with your instructor, then you are not fully taking advantage of the time you spent doing the homework in the first place.

As for the second point, homework often counts as a portion of your grade. As a result, not doing it should NEVER be an option. Regardless of how long it takes, you just need to do it. In many cases, you have time during class to get started on it. It amazed me how many times students did not take advantage of this. When free time was given in class, they would draw pictures in their notebooks, write love letters, or simply just stare into space. Why not take advantage of that time? My mindset was that since I had to be in class anyway, I should work on homework as much as possible so that I can spend less time working on it at home. Don't underestimate the value of doing this. If you start your homework in class, you can get feedback or help from your instructor before taking it home and potentially getting stuck and having to wait until the following class to get help.

Homework also directly prepares you for quizzes and exams. In almost all cases, the questions and problems you do as part of your homework, will reappear in one form or fashion on a quiz or exam. Granted, there will be times when you are assigned "busy work" that won't truly prepare you for an exam. While this can be frustrating, you still need to do it for the obvious reason of not losing points but also for the reasons below.

Not doing homework also does irreparable damage to your reputation as a student. It tells the teacher that you simply don't care or that school isn't important to you. Besides the obvious fact of directly impacting your grade, the teacher/

professor will be less likely to want to help you should you need some help down the road. His/her mindset will be: why should I go out of my way to help you when you don't even do your homework. In addition, in many subjects, a great deal of the material is graded subjectively. When this is the case, you are more likely to get the benefit of the doubt if you are a hard working student who always turns in his/her homework on time. For example, if you miss a homework assignment from time to time and your final average is an 89, you are less likely to be bumped up to a 90 then you would be if you never missed a homework assignment. Another way of thinking about it is that homework is all about effort. The instructor isn't always concerned with whether or not you got everything correct. They are more concerned with whether or not you really tried to get through the assignment. Simply put, just do your home-work. You will better off because of it.

CHAPTER 7

Just Say No

When it comes to commitment and discipline, being able to "say no" is one of the most difficult things for us to do. It is human nature to choose the easier path or to do things that give us pleasure versus doing those things that are difficult or take time and concentration. In order to "say no", you have to tell yourself over and over again that the results will far outweigh the sadness over missing out on something fun. On the other hand, it is very important to have a good student/life/work balance. When you do have free time, you need to make it a priority to enjoy yourself and engage in some of those pleasures you may miss out on from time to time.

This principle applies as early as middle school. As a 6th or 7th grader, I really enjoyed watching Monday Night Football. However, if I had an exam the next day or had a paper due, I had to sacrifice the football game and make sure I did what I had to do in order to prepare. At that age, many believe that it is the parents' responsibility to make sure their children do what they need to do to succeed in school. Although I don't disagree with that statement, I believe that the earlier a student can develop self-discipline, the better off he or she will be in the long run. As a side benefit, it helps the parents, who no longer have to "hover over" the student to make sure everything gets done. In return, the student will really enjoy their parents not bugging them every day about school. During middle and high school, I can honestly say that my parents didn't ask me about school or get on me about my grades or assignments one time. I made sure things got done and that I was always prepared for what was coming.

While it was challenging as a junior high student, it really only meant missing a television show or two, a sleepover, or maybe a trip to the movies. As you get older this becomes more and more difficult. In high school, it takes serious discipline to be able to tell your best friends "no". Initially, they may make fun of you or give you a hard time. However, over time, it has been my experience that they respect you more because of it and wish they had the same commitment level as you. Growing up in New Orleans, you can only imagine the kinds of things that I had to pass up from time to time. I remember missing some huge parties, crazy nights on Bourbon Street, LSU football games, and even a few fishing trips. However, when it was all said and done, I was the one with the scholarship offers to college whereas many of my peers were simply trying to figure out how they would get in or pay for it.

Although all of the things above did happen from time to time, I made a conscious effort to get the most out of the time I had available during the week or during the daytime hours on the weekend so that I didn't have to miss out on the fun opportunities. I believe it is essential to be able to blow off some steam from time to time and really have fun. If not, you will get burned out and will not be able to keep this commitment. While the message here is to "say no", the key is to only have to do so when there are no other options. If you know you have a huge paper that is due on Friday and there is a big party on Thursday night, it goes without saying that you need to do everything you can to finish the paper prior to Thursday night.

Once I got to college, this was THE number one thing that allowed me to keep my GPA as high as I did. In college, unlike high school, there are things going on every night of the week both on and off campus. There are enough distractions to keep even the most disciplined person on his/her toes. As a college freshman, you can easily be overwhelmed by the entire experience and it is vital that you get your arms around it. It only takes one bad semester to really put a kink into all of your future plans. I know someone very well who had good grades in college except for one really bad semester. That semester has basically prevented her from getting into nursing school, dental hygiene school, and from pursuing several other career paths. She has told me countless times how much she wished she could have a "do over" and how that one semester basically ruined her academically. As hard as it is, being able to "say no" can truly prevent this dilemma and help you keep your priorities in order.

When should you say no? In my mind, this is simple. When you get invited to go to a party, go on a road trip, or go to a concert, look yourself in the mirror and ask yourself if this event will prevent you from doing the best you can on any upcoming work, exams, paper, etc. If it will have little to no effect, then by all means go. However, if you even have to think twice about it, I think you know what the answer is. You can easily come up with arguments to convince yourself otherwise, but your gut instinct will tell you all you need to know.

CHAPTER 8

Study Time

The duration of time needed to study will always differ from one student to the next based on a number of variables including but not limited to one's natural ability to retain information, grasp difficult concepts, etc. However, where, when, and how you study can be chosen by all of us and I strongly believe that you can use these three factors to your advantage and shorten the time it will take for you to comprehend, retain, and understand the subject matter at hand. As has been the theme throughout this book, the quality of study time is much more important than the quantity of study time.

When it comes to studying for a large exam or test, I am convinced that the best way to do so is in absolute silence. I know there are plenty of folks who study while listening to music or the television. This doesn't make sense to me. Either do one or the other. If you are doing either of the things mentioned above, you are "wasting" some of your senses on stimuli that are counterproductive to what you are trying to do. Even if you think you can study and do both, your brain is still processing what you are hearing or seeing. When it comes time to studying, find the quietest place possible. Whereas younger students really don't have much choice in where they study, high school and college students have many options.

Finding a good place to study can be very difficult for a number of reasons. There are distractions everywhere you turn such as cell phones ringing, dogs barking, siblings crying, visitors coming to the house, mom and dad arguing, etc. During my younger years, I had no choice but to study at home and the noise was unbearable. As a result, I turned to another variable I mentioned earlier and that was WHEN I studied. While it may seem a bit radical, I started studying for exams in the morning before school. Depending on how many hours I thought I needed to study, I would set my alarm that many hours ahead of when I would usually wake up. You wouldn't believe how quiet the house is at 3am. I would wake up, take a shower, drink a Coke, and then hit the books.

After doing this a few times, I realized that I had stumbled upon something extraordinary. The time I spent studying was free of all distractions. In addition, I no longer had to yell at my brothers and parents when I was trying to study in the evenings. I was also able to retain information better because sleep did not occur between the time I studied and the exam. While I don't profess to be an expert in neuroscience, I do know that it is easier to retain information throughout the woken hours than it is to retain it after a long sleep. In middle and high school, since so much of the exams covered vocabulary, events, dates, lists, acronyms etc, this was a huge advantage. When studying during traditional hours, I found I was losing some retention overnight. With this new method, this was no longer an issue.

Once I entered college, studying sometimes entailed more than just a few hours. When this was the case, I still studied in the middle of the night when all was quiet. However, when one morning wasn't enough to cut it and I needed to study in the afternoons or evenings, I found that the library cubicles were the best place to study on campus. It was quiet there and you had ample space to spread your books out.

Another important strategy I used was to not study for more than an hour or so without taking a short break. I found that once I spent an hour of intense studying, I started to lose focus. As a result, I would always take a short break of 5 minutes or so every hour to get something to drink, get a bite to eat, get up and stretch, etc. I can still picture some of those mornings in college when I couldn't wait until my 7am break because that was when the cafeteria opened and I would take a break for breakfast. I would then come back, finish my studying and go take my exam at 8 or 9am, depending on the particular class I was taking.

On nights that I knew I would be getting up really early for an exam, I would try to go to sleep as early as possible, sometimes at 8pm or so. These were the nights when I would have to tell my friends I couldn't go out with them because I had to get up early and study for an exam. On many occasions, I was up studying the next morning when they were just coming back from a night of partying. What was so interesting was that most of my peers would spend days and days studying for an exam whereas I would only study for a few hours that morning and 9 times out of 10, I scored better than they did. I don't think it was because I was any smarter. I do believe it was because I took better notes, paid more attention in class, and studied with far less (if any) distractions.

As for how I spent my time studying, it depended on the subject matter at hand. For math courses, the studying revolved around reviewing the various problems we covered in class, reviewing notes at a high level, and actually doing some of the problems at the end of each chapter. In most math textbooks, they usually contain chapter reviews, for which answers can be found in the back of the book. To me, math courses were the easiest to study for because once you got the concepts down in class, it was just repetition. In addition (again, no pun intended), you have the opportunity to practically take the test beforehand based on the problem types reviewed in class and at the end of the chapters. It was extremely rare for me to come across a problem on a test for which I had not seen a similar problem in class or in homework. To succeed in math, the key once again is to never go into a test or an exam without knowing how to solve a particular type of problem. Odds are that problem type was covered in class and if you don't understand how to solve it, there really is no excuse. In a previous chapter, I mentioned how important it was to ask questions and to seek out help so that you understand the topic at hand. When it comes to math, the only points you should lose on a test are those made due to simple mistakes. You should never miss a question because you have no idea how to do it.

Generally speaking, I studied for all of the other subjects basically the same way. My notes were the primary focus. I spent those uninterrupted, distraction-free moments reviewing my notes page by page. I was sure to review those items I had underlined, marked with an asterisk, or highlighted with even more focus. If there were acronyms, lists, or other things that needed to be memorized, I would quiz myself over and over again until I got it 100% correct. If the exam covered chapters from a text book, I would also review the chapter summaries looking for those key points that I may have missed in my notes. In addition, I was sure to review any handouts that were given during class. Very seldom will an instructor hand out something to review and not cover it on some sort of assessment. Last, if the teacher gave out a study guide or review sheet, that would take even more precedence over my notes since any notes having nothing to do with any of the topics on the review sheet/study guide could be ignored. For most assessments, I would go through all of my material twice just to make sure I had a good handle on everything. This could take anywhere from an hour or two up to five or six hours depending on the subject and the amount of material covered.

While the time it takes for you to master the material may differ in length from what I describe above, I firmly believe that it will work for you. Obviously, the what, when, and how you study plays an enormous role in how you fare on quizzes, tests, and exams. As mentioned earlier, what you do in the

classroom is equally as important. If you treat each component with the dedication, commitment, and discipline needed,
the sky is the limit for what you can achieve.

CHAPTER 9

Flying Solo

During my time in college and graduate school, one of the things that blew my mind was how much stock people put into group studying. I think the appeal comes from the idea that by studying in a group, each individual will learn what the group collectively knows. While this would be effective if playing a game of Trivial Pursuit, I firmly believe that group study is one of the worst ways to spend your precious time preparing for an exam. I am not only saying this based on opinion alone. I actually tried it on several occasions and I only found it marginally helpful. Don't get me wrong. It can be a lot of fun, and it is much more enjoyable than spending the night or the early hours in the library preparing for an exam alone. However, it is NOT a very efficient way to study and it will not produce the results you want.

Based on the few times that I tried it, there was very little studying and much more laughing, gossiping, and making weekend plans. Sure there were topics and review questions sprinkled in between some of the immaterial comments. As time passed, I found myself aggravated by the fact that what the group covered in a couple of hours, I could have covered in 30 minutes alone. It only took a couple of these experiences to convince me that this was not the way to go. My opinion was later bolstered by the fact that on the next couple of tests, I scored significantly higher than some of my group-studying peers did. To put the icing on the cake, I later found out that they had "studied" all night long when I had only put in a couple of hours. If you are fully prepared for an exam, and you want to join the group for more of a social experience and some additional review, then I would say go for it. However, if you are truly trying to prepare, flying solo is absolutely the way to go.

Part IV:

Student/Life/Work Balance

CHAPTER 10

SMART Goals

Goal setting played a huge role in my success as a student and continues to do so in my role at the office. Whether it is setting yearly, monthly, weekly, daily, or in some cases hourly goals, they help keep you focused on and motivated by the task at hand. Goal achievement gives you a sense of accomplishment, builds confidence, and allows you to reflect back on what you have done and be proud of it. Whenever you consider creating a goal, it is very important that it has certain characteristics. For those of you who have heard of SMART goals, this may be a review. For those who have not, SMART stands for Specific, Measurable, Achievable, Realistic, and Timed. I will examine each characteristic in more detail so that you have a good understanding of how each contributes to good goal setting.

Goals need to be "specific". If they are too general, they begin to become very unmanageable and therefore, lose its purpose. In addition, you can play mind games with yourself and twist things around so that you can tell yourself you met a particular goal when you really did not. In this case, you would only be kidding yourself. For example, you may set a goal to make better grades for next semester. Well, what does that mean? Does that mean that you need to improve in every subject matter? Does it mean that you want your final exams to be better? If you make a very high grade on the first exam, did you meet your goal? A more specific goal would be to improve your GPA for the next semester from a 3.0 to a 3.5. This characteristic ties in very nicely to the next one.

In my mind, being "measurable" is the most important characteristic of any goal. Specific goals are much easier to measure than more general goals. For example, a manager may have a goal for his employees to be happier. For one, that goal isn't very specific. To make matters worse, it is almost impossible to measure. A better goal for that manager would be to increase his team's scores on the employee opinion survey by 15% compared to last year's survey scores. The survey is a measure of employee happiness and now he can actually assess whether or not he met his goal. Whenever you set a goal, ask yourself how you are going to measure it. If you can't come up with an answer, you most likely need to adjust your goal.

The next two characteristics, "achievable and realistic", describe basically the same thing. In my mind, I believe both are simply included to make the acronym easy to remember. A good goal is realistic. While it should push and motivate you towards accomplishment, it shouldn't be so extreme that your chances of reaching it are one in a million. For example, it would not be a good idea to have a goal of buying a brand new Lamborghini right out of college. While it would be awesome to reach that goal, it is not very realistic and therefore, in almost all cases, you are setting yourself up for failure or disappointment. A more realistic goal would be to purchase a new Ford Mustang after graduation. When it comes to your grades, set goals that are attainable yet push you quite a bit. If you reach those, you can always set your sights higher the next time.

The last characteristic is "timed". In my opinion, this characteristic is second only to a goal being measurable. All good goals have some type of time component tied to it. Besides giving you some type of deadline, it gives you a definite point at which you can assess the goal and determine whether or not you have hit it. Let's say you have a goal to have a million dollars in the bank. My next question would be "by when?" If you can't answer the "when" question when examining your goal, it most likely is missing the time component and needs to be amended. A better goal is to have one million dollars in the bank by age 55. While this goal now meets all of the characteristics of a SMART goal, it may need some interval goals to check progress. If I set that goal at age 35, I may want to set additional goals to have $250K by 40 and $500K by 47 to check my progress. If I set that goal now and have to wait 20 years to see how I am doing, I may very easily lose sight of it.

So, how does this apply to the classroom? Setting SMART goals can really keep you on track each and every day. You can set goals for the year, the semester, the 6 weeks, the final exam, or even for the next assignment. You can set goals for how you will study for a particular exam, write a term paper, or even how you will spend the weekend. For example, while studying, you may set a small goal to get through Chapters 1, 2, and 3 before taking a 10 minute break. You could set a goal to have your term paper done by Noon on Saturday so that you will have the rest of the weekend to hang out with your friends. When you reach these goals, you will have a sense of accomplishment and feel good that you were able to do what you set out to do. This applies to very small mundane tasks all the way up to very difficult projects. The process is the same. The only difference is that for the larger projects, you can have smaller goals or checkpoints along the way to make sure you are where you need to be. Goal setting goes hand in hand with the next topic to be covered, which is time management.

CHAPTER 11

Time Management

Time is a gift that all of us have. However, how we use this time is what sets us apart from one another. When it comes to managing your academics, athletics, hobbies, social life, et cetera, time management is essential. It is what allows us to keep a balanced lifestyle. Too much of anything is seldom good. I have found that by using SMART goals on a day to day basis, you can really manage your time and get the most out of life while still achieving great things inside and outside the classroom.

Your ability to manage your time in middle school and junior high is very dependent on your parents. Since you can't drive yet, there are many times when you are totally dependent on their schedules. However, you do control what you do after you get home from school each day as well as what you do on most weekends. At this age, my strategy was primarily to do my homework early in the mornings before school so I could stay outside and play with my friends after school. Besides, I always had some type of athletic practice after school, which meant I didn't get home until dinner time on most nights.

In high school, especially once you are of driving age, you have a little more control over your time. There are tons of distractions and many reasons why you will be tempted to put off studying or doing your homework until the last minute or even not doing it at all. It is imperative to not fall into this trap. Set small goals to do those things you need to do and try to get them out of the way as quickly as possible to leave more time for the things you really want to do. While I feel I am a very good at multi-tasking, I have always found it more efficient to "dedicate" time to a particular effort until the task is completed rather than trying to manage multiple tasks at the same time. For example, let's say you have a test tomorrow and there is a TV show you really want to watch at 9pm. I would try to get all my homework done after dinner in plenty enough time for the show. If you try to do your homework while watching TV, the quality of your work will go down and you won't be able to truly enjoy your TV show. Today, your best bet would be to set the DVR and watch it when you did have free time. Of course, I could have set the VHS recorder back in the 80's and 90's, but that was much more difficult and really wasn't worth all of the effort.

Another strategy I always used and continue to employ today is to never sit idle. There is always something you can be doing such as chores, homework, spending time with friends or family, etc. If you do need some down time, plan for it and feel good about just sitting back and relaxing. The problem is folks do this when there are tons of more useful things they could be doing. Most school-aged kids don't realize how much time they have. If you can't manage time at this age when you have less things going on, it will be extremely difficult in high school, college and beyond.

College presents a whole new set of challenges when it comes to time management. You have the ability to schedule when you go to class, when you go to work, when to party, when to take road trips, etc. Time management, commitment, and discipline all come into play when it comes to being a successful college student. I believe that it all starts with scheduling your classes. Whether you or a morning person or an evening person, I strongly suggest bundling all of your classes sequentially (without breaks except for lunch) to get the most of the time you have. For example, if you are a morning person, I suggest taking back to back to back classes, break for lunch, and then take another class or two. This is very advantageous as it bundles all of your class time together so that once class is over for the day, you can concentrate on all of the other things you have going on. On the other hand, if you take a class at 8am and then another at 10am and another at 3pm, it is broken up throughout the day and in many cases you don't have enough time in between to accomplish much else. That time basically gets eaten away with a half hour here and an hour or so there. When I was an undergrad, I tried the best I could to start class at 8am and be done by 1 or 2pm. This allowed me to get all of my classes out of the way so that I could concentrate on football during the fall semester and track and field in the spring semester. It also gave me enough time in between school and practice to get other things done or to even take a nap, especially if it was one of those mornings when I had been up since 3am studying for a major exam. Most of my friends scheduled classes at all different times throughout the day and while they had some breaks, they were never really done and had to manage the rest of their lives in between classes. In most cases, you should be able to schedule your classes using this strategy. However, there will be times when you cannot, such as when you need to take a particular class and it is only offered at one time. In this case, you do the best you can with your schedule to make it work for you.

Another thing that worked well for me was getting into a routine. Humans are creatures of habit and if you can get into the routine of doing things over and over again at the same time of the day, you can plan for things outside of your routine. If done well, you can make sure there is plenty of time for fun, parties, social time, and relaxation. Almost every day in the spring my friends and I would play basketball in the gym, go swimming, play a game of touch football, etc. We would take a break in the early evening to get some work done and then we would hang out for a bit before going to bed. If you can take anything away any from this, it is to plan as much as possible. I really try to live by the saying "if you fail to plan, you plan to fail". That is what time management is all about. It really allows you to fit in as much as possible with the time you have every day. Sure there will be times when sleep is sacrificed, but when it is, you need to try to figure out when you can catch up as too much sleep deprivation can cause its own set of problems.

Every day you wake up, you should think about what you want or need to accomplish that day both from an academic and leisure perspective. One tool that really helped me was the "list". I would wake up and jot down the things that I really wanted to get done that day. It could be assignments, study time, running errands, calling home, etc. The important thing was to write it down. By the end of the day, you could strike through those things you accomplished and carry over the ones you didn't onto tomorrow's list. Using the list, I determined what I could do with the time I had throughout the day. In many cases, I would prioritize the list so I knew what took precedence over the other tasks. Obviously, things will and do come up unexpectedly. When this occurs, just re-prioritize your list and keep moving.

Time management isn't something you can master right away. However, with practice, you will get better and better and before you know it, you won't believe how much more you can accomplish each day compared to when you weren't making a conscious effort to manage your time wisely.

CHAPTER 12

Celebrate

I want to end by talking about how important it is to celebrate throughout your academic journey and beyond. While I have spent the previous 11 chapters talking about discipline, commitment, being able to say no, time management, etc., it is equally important to celebrate your victories, both large and small. To achieve student/life balance, it is important that you spend quality time with your friends and family. To do so, you need to make sure that you plan for and allocate time for those fun activities. In some cases, you may even refer to it as blowing off some steam.

This can even be applied to small day to day victories. If you finish your homework early, go play a video game or talk to friends about the upcoming weekend. Jump on the various social media outlets and see what is going on. The key here is to find time for enjoyment along the way. While everyone knows it isn't a good idea to be a full blown party animal, it is equally as important to not be totally consumed by your studies. Social activities are extremely important for that student/

life/work balance and you must dedicate ample time to it as well. All of the things discussed previously aim at giving you all the tools you need to be very successful in the classroom without having to dedicate all of your time outside the classroom. I challenge you to try what you have learned in this book for a semester or two and see how it works for you. You may determine that some of the things work really well for you and some do not. Even if you only take away one thing that helps you, it will have been worth your time and energy used to read this. Good luck and remember that nothing worthwhile comes easy. If you are going to do something, jump in with both feet, give it your all, and let the pieces fall where they may. You will be comforted by the fact that you did the best that you could, regardless of the result.

Good Luck!

Printed in Great Britain
by Amazon